P9-DSV-318

ODD SCIENCE

HUMAN BODY

James Olstein

STERLING CHILDREN'S BOOKS
New York

Our bodies are fascinating, from the atoms that form us to the energy that we create, from the bones that hold us up to the bacteria that call our bodies home.

Human bodies have all kinds of strange secrets, such as stomach acid that can dissolve metal, a liver that can regenerate itself, and small cells that eat debris in the brain.

This book will reveal things you have never heard before. It will tell you unknown facts about our bodies themselves, but it will also surprise you with facts about the body's reactions to the things you love, such as music, exercise, and ice cream.

This book will tell you the true size of the human brain, why you cannot tickle yourself (no matter how hard you try), and how much snot your body can make in one day—disgusting!

Quirky, strange, and cool—come inside the world of odd science.

---

*Special thanks to Neil Dunnicliffe and Hattie Grylls.
None of the Odd Science books would be
possible without you.*

CONTENTS

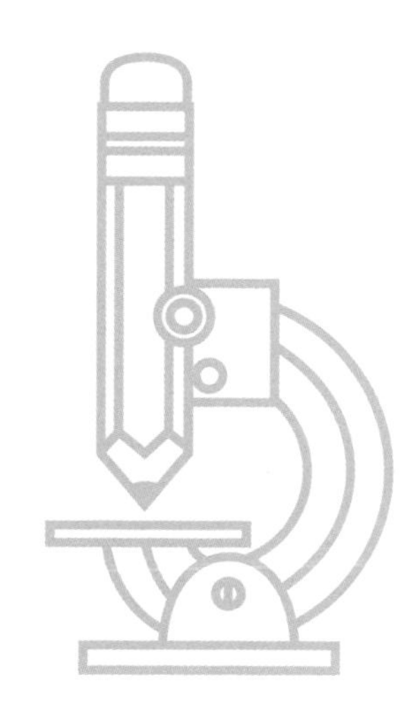

ON THE BLOCK

A person is made out of tiny building blocks called atoms. There are around 7 octillion atoms inside each adult body. That is a staggering 7,000,000,000,000,000,000,000,000,000!

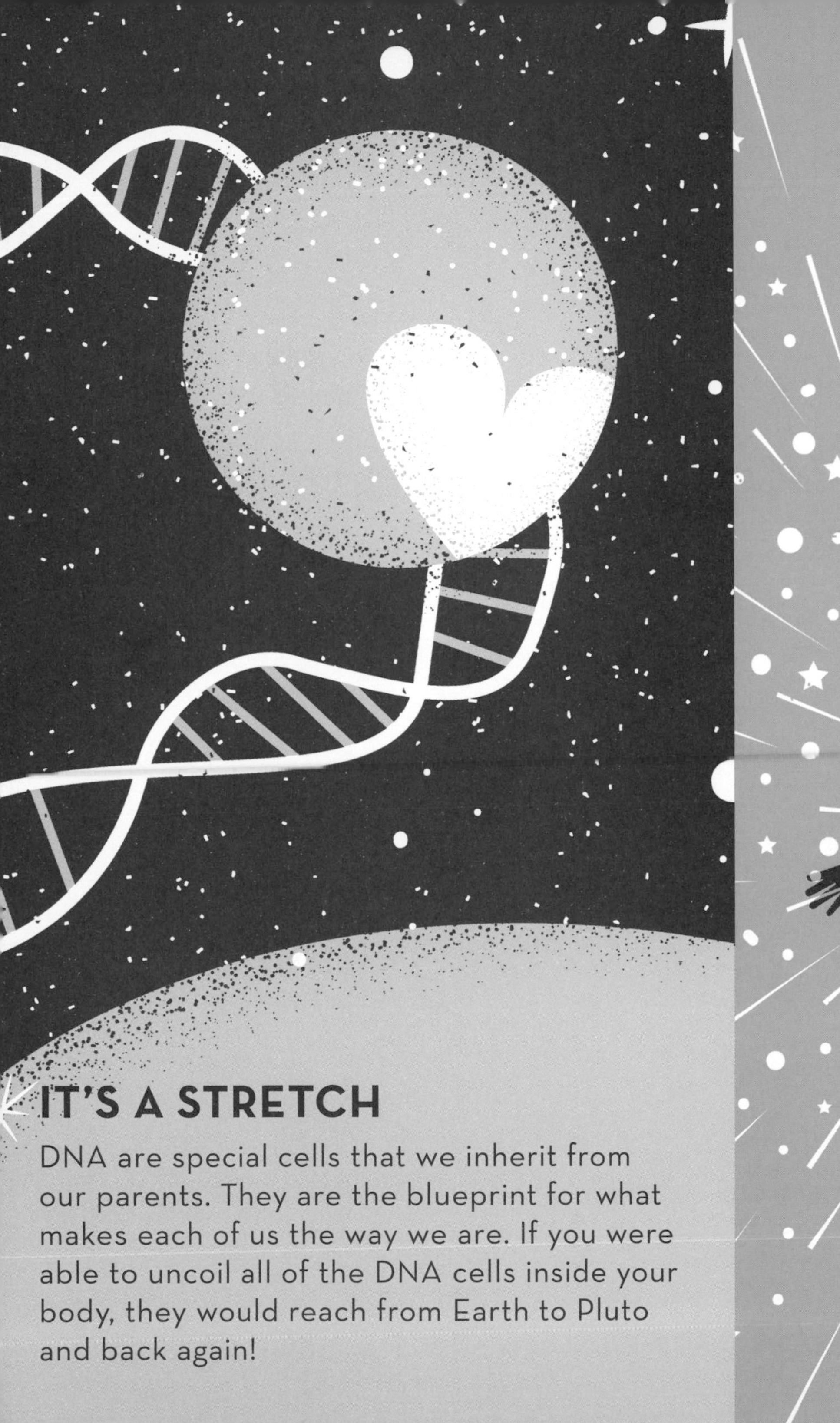

IT'S A STRETCH

DNA are special cells that we inherit from our parents. They are the blueprint for what makes each of us the way we are. If you were able to uncoil all of the DNA cells inside your body, they would reach from Earth to Pluto and back again!

YOU'RE A STAR!

We each have a little stardust inside us. When giant stars explode, they eject elements, such as iron and calcium, into space. These elements join new matter, including stars, while some mix with planets, such as Earth. The iron in our blood and the calcium in our bones originated from these explosions.

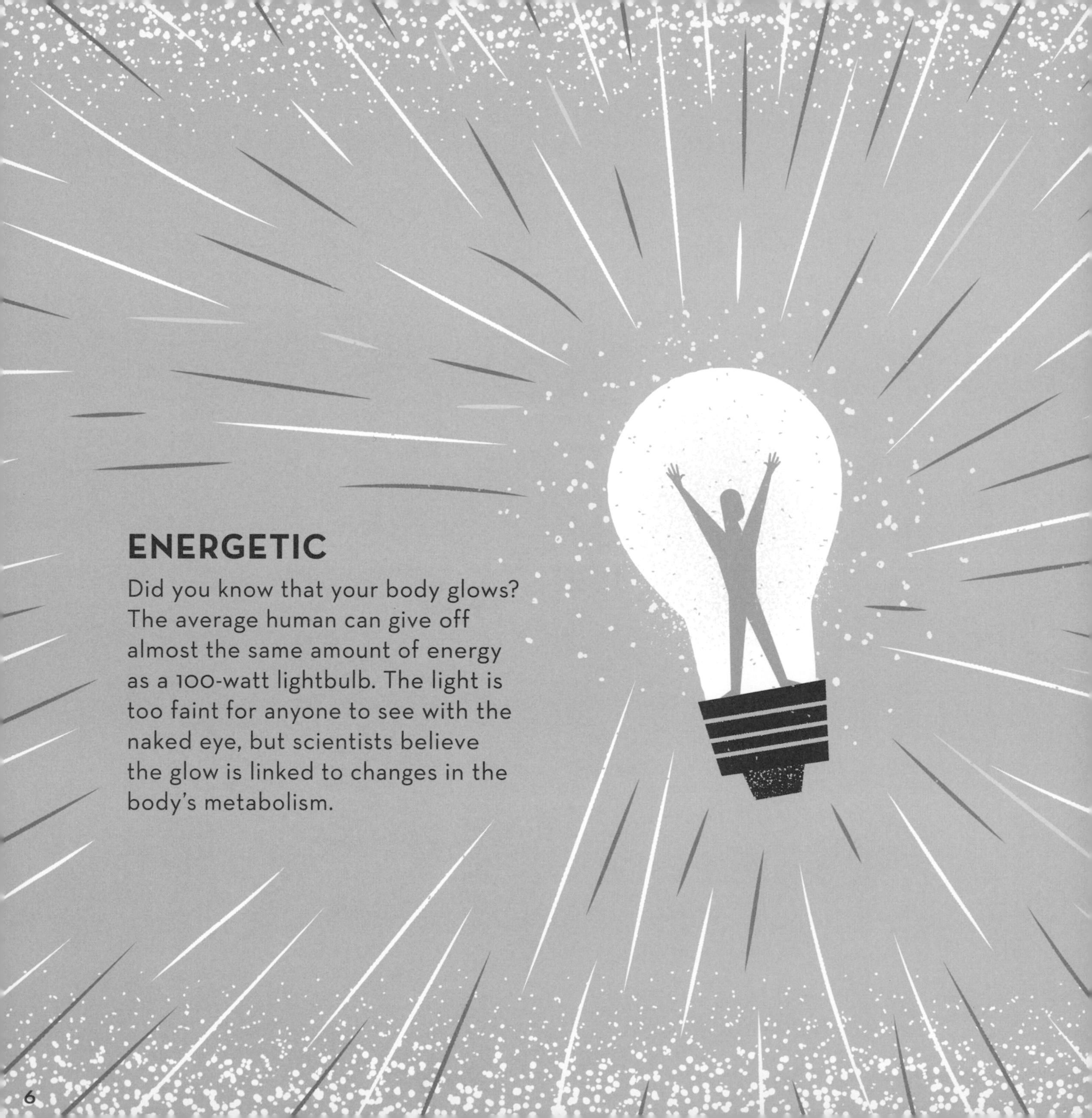

ENERGETIC

Did you know that your body glows? The average human can give off almost the same amount of energy as a 100-watt lightbulb. The light is too faint for anyone to see with the naked eye, but scientists believe the glow is linked to changes in the body's metabolism.

KEEP ON TRUCKING!

Every day, your heart creates enough energy to power a truck for 20 miles.

POT OF GOLD

Many people get the holes in their teeth filled in with gold or other precious metals. Over time, however, small amounts of these fillings are swallowed down with food and drink. What goes in must come out and, as a result, human sewage contains tiny pieces of gold, silver, and other rare metals.

NAILED IT!

There can be up to 1/64 ounce of iron in your bloodstream. That's enough to forge a small nail.

GOLD-ILOCKS

There are more than 100 confirmed elements in the periodic table, and 60 of those can be found in our bodies. Your hair, for example, contains traces of gold. Gold exists naturally as nanoparticles in Earth's soil as well as in seawater. Plants and animals absorb some of these tiny particles and pass them up the food chain to us.

HAIRY BUSINESS

A full head of healthy human hair is strong enough to support an estimated 13.22 tons. That is the weight of two elephants!

FUR-IOUS

A human's body has as many hairs per square inch as many other mammals, but it normally is unnoticed, because the strands are fine. Other mammals tend to be covered in a thicker coat of fur that sheds regularly.

HAIRY NUMBERS

The thickness of your hair can be determined by its color. Typically, blonds have the densest hair.

TAKES A LOT OF NERVE

Your brain has more than 86 billion nerve cells inside it, which are linked by 100 trillion connections. There are many more connections inside our heads than there are stars in our galaxy, the Milky Way.

WRINKLE IN TIME

The human brain is so wrinkled that two-thirds of it is hidden within the folds. If you could iron your brain so that it is flat, it would spread across more than $2\frac{2}{3}$ square feet. Your brain is the body's most complex organ. As you get older, the fibers inside the brain grow, making it become even more wrinkled.

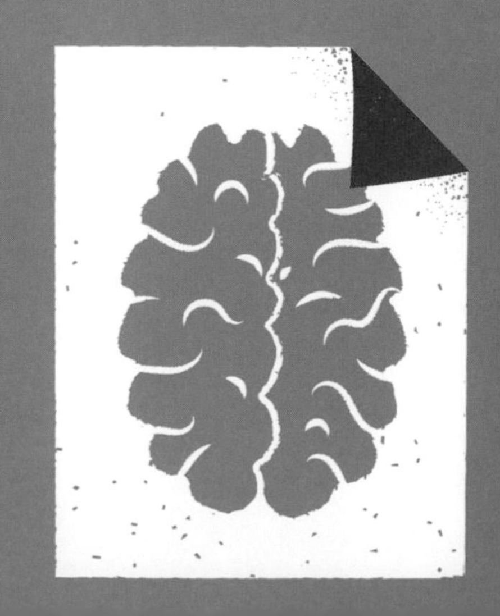

WATER LOG

Your brain is made up of more than 73 percent water. The liquid inside helps it with the important work of sending electric signals all over the body.

FREEZE!

Sphenopalatine ganglioneuralgia, also known as brain freeze, is a type of alarm the brain gives off when you eat or drink something that is icy cold. The frosty snack causes the brain's blood vessels to contract too quickly, resulting in a headache.

BRAIN DRAIN

Thinking is hard work. About 20 percent of your entire body's oxygen and food intake is used to power the brain. Sometimes there is so much processing to do, the brain becomes even more active when you are asleep than when you are awake.

FAST FILTER

Your brain takes in 11 million pieces of information every second, but it only consciously processes about 40 of those pieces.

NO PAIN, ALL BRAIN

The brain is an amazing tool that can detect pain signals coming from all over the body. The organ itself, however, cannot feel pain. Headaches are caused when pain receptors in the skull, neck, and other areas around the brain become aggravated.

BRAIN GAMES

Microglia are small cells that eat debris and material that no longer functions in our brain. Scientists have used the video game Pac-Man to explain how the microalgia move around our heads gobbling up the bad stuff.

MEGABYTES

The average home computer holds between 250 and 320 gigabytes of memory, but the human brain contains more than a million. If its storage capacity could be converted into an electrical device, the brain would be able to hold 3 million hours of television shows. They would need to run constantly for more than 300 years before its memory was used up.

NEUR-RUN

Nerve impulses can travel to and from the brain at incredible speeds, with some reaching more than 250 miles per hour. That is faster than a Formula One racing car.

IT TAKES TWO

It is impossible to tickle yourself, no matter how hard you try. Part of the physical reaction to being tickled is caused by the surprise.

IN THE BLINK OF AN EYE

The fastest reacting muscle you have is the one that makes each of your eyes blink. It can close the eye in less that one-hundredth of a second.

EYE-EYE!

The only part of the body that does not have any blood vessels is the cornea—the colorless, dome-shaped surface that covers the eye. It gets its oxygen directly from the air.

FOCUS GROUP

The muscles that focus your eyes move more than three times in a second. That is about 100,000 times a day.

COLOR PALETTE

Your awesome eyes can distinguish between approximately 10 million different shades of color.

EYE-CON

If your eye was a digital camera, it would have a resolution of 576 megapixels.

EYE CARUMBA!

Eyes reach their maximum size when we become teenagers, yet our noses and ears appear to get bigger as we age. Scientists are still trying to agree why this happens, although gravity seems to be a big factor.

WAXY WOES

Your ears secrete more earwax when you are afraid. Wax production is controlled by the apocrine glands, which are also responsible for making sweat. The glands cause the ears to make extra wax at these times in the same way that we sweat more when we are scared.

WASTE DISPOSAL

As well as keeping your airways moist, the mucus inside your nose is there to catch germs and dirt. When you breathe in air, the mucus gets dried out and becomes hard, turning it into a booger. It is just your body's way of ridding itself of unwanted trash.

SNOT WHAT YOU THINK

Mucus is so important to the function of your nose, your body makes a new batch every 20 minutes. The human body produces about 1 quart of mucus per day.

HEAVEN SCENT

Scientists have deduced that the human nose can sniff out the difference between at least a trillion different odors.

WHO NOSE HOW FAST

The air from a human sneeze can exceed speeds of 100 miles per hour. Even a cough can reach 50 miles per hour.

FRESH SCENT

Humans have their own, unique smell. Even newborn babies can recognize the individual scent of their mama.

DROOL POOL

All day long, our bodies swallow and then reabsorb saliva. The flow production ranges between 4¼ cups and 8½ cups a day. In a lifetime, that is enough spit to fill 53 bathtubs, or about a 50-by-100-foot swimming pool.

PERSON OF TASTE

A new taste can be identified in less than one-five hundredth, or 0.0015, of a second—faster than it takes to blink an eye. To be able to properly taste a food or liquid, however, your saliva has to dissolve it first.

DON'T EAT ME BRO(MELAIN)

Has your mouth ever hurt while eating a pineapple? It is the fault of an enzyme inside the fruit called bromelain. Bromelain digests proteins, so the pineapple is effectively eating you back as you munch away.

TOOTHACHE

Tooth enamel is made up of 90 percent minerals—not cells or proteins like the rest of the body. They are the only part of you that is unable to repair itself.

BABY TEETH

The teeth in your mouth started growing six months before you were born. One out of every 2,000 newborn infants comes into the world with one or more teeth already visible.

TOOTHFULLY

Did you know that your teeth are just as hard as those of a shark? The enamel coating on a shark's impressive fangs is no tougher than the enamel that covers yours.

ON THE TIP OF MY TONGUE

No one in the world has the same tongue print as you. Its unique set of bumps and ridges can be used to pick you out from a crowd, just like a fingerprint.

ALL SMILES

At a minimum, it takes 10 of the 43 muscles in the face to smile, but only 6 muscles to frown.

TRUNK CLUB

Your tongue is a muscular hydrostat—a densely packed array of muscles that are not supported by a rigid bone structure. The trunk of an elephant is a muscular hydrostat, too.

SMALL ONLY IN NAME

Contrary to what you might think, the longest part of the body is actually the small intestine. When uncoiled, it measures between 20 feet and 25 feet.

BREAKING THE SOUND BARRIER

The world record for the loudest burp ever recorded reached a thundering 109.9 decibels, which is louder than a jet taking off.

BETTER OUT THAN IN

During the digestive process, gas naturally builds up inside the stomach and then gets released as a burp. Farts come from gas built up inside the intestines, as the bacteria digests food even further. On average, a healthy person will break wind around 14 times a day, although they do not always hear or smell the evidence.

GAS UP

Each day, your body can produce enough gas to fill up a birthday balloon.

HEAVYWEIGHT

In its lifetime, the human body will process about 38.5 tons of food.

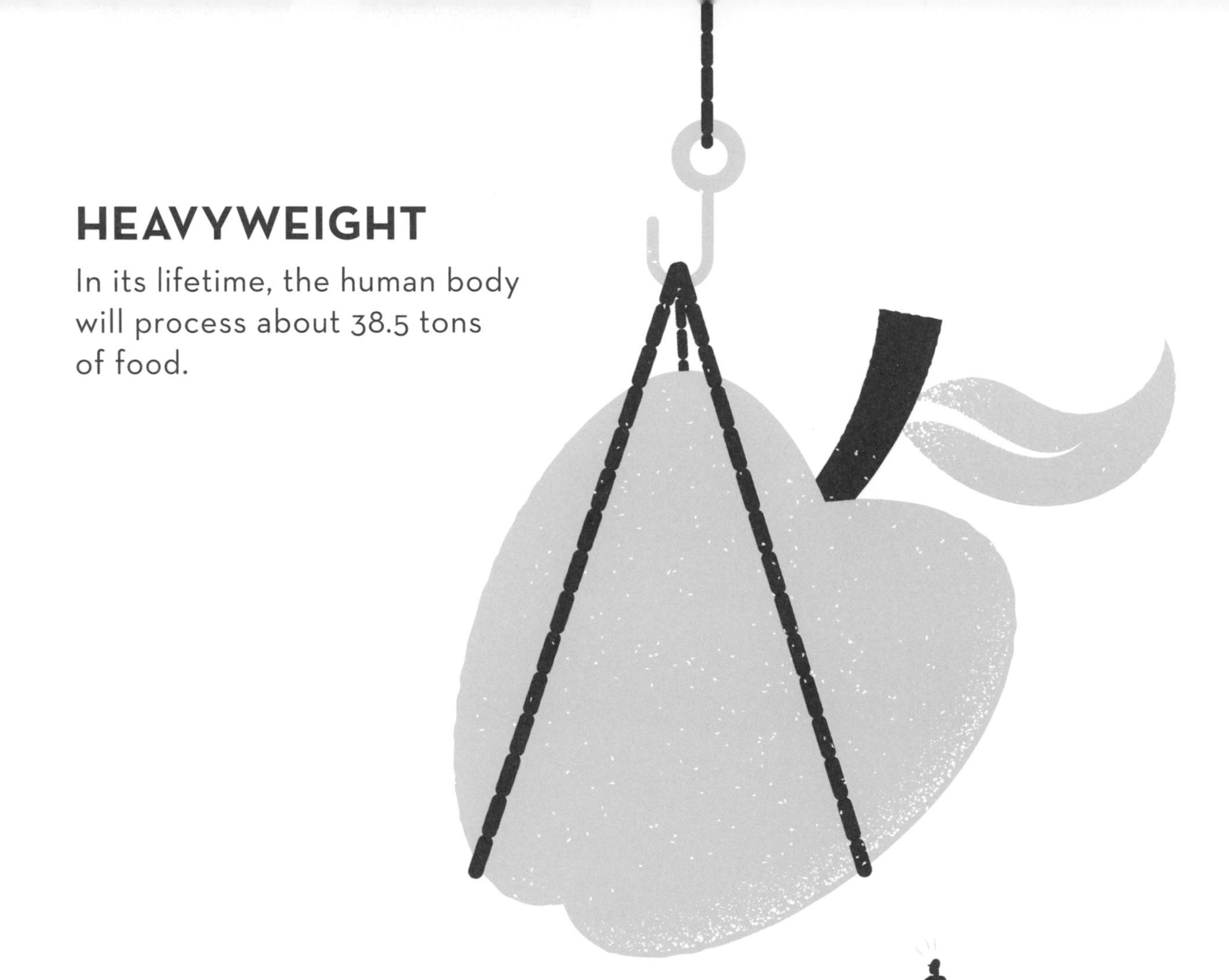

HAPPY MEAL

Scientists have discovered that food can directly affect our mood. People who eat healthy, nutritious meals tend to be more content.

GRRRRRRRRRRR

Why does your stomach growl? It's just the sound of your stomach muscles contracting as it prepares for food. The scientific name for the rumbles is borborygmus.

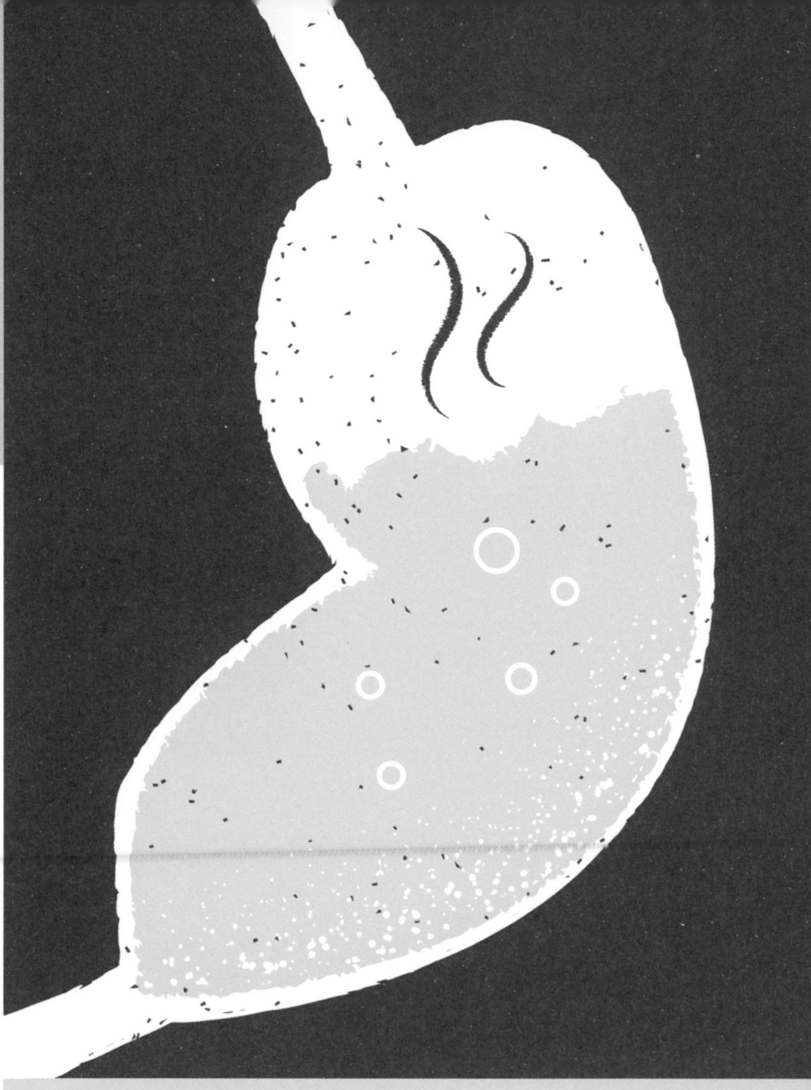

DEADLY ACID

Your stomach is filled with acid that is powerful enough to dissolve metal. The cells of your stomach wall are constantly renewing themselves to keep the acid from hurting you.

NO GRAZING

Unlike cows, humans cannot digest grass. Our bodies do not have what it takes to break down the cellulose found inside the plant.

WHAT'S UP?

When you eat, the muscles in your esophagus tighten and loosen in waves, pushing food down into your stomach. This is known as peristalsis. Even if you were hanging upside down, your body would still be able to move food to your stomach, because it does not need gravity to help get it there.

POOP SCOOP

The waste we eject from our bodies is not just a mix of food and water—it also contains other matter, such as bile from the liver and old red blood cells. This combination gives poop its brown color.

PANDA-MONIUM

It is estimated that an adult human will produce around 320 pounds of poop in a single year. That's heavier than an adult panda bear.

IT TAKES GUTS

When you ride a fast roller coaster, do you sometimes get the feeling that your stomach is jumping up into your throat? That's because some internal organs shift and become slightly weightless due to the motion of the ride.

NO KIDNEY-ING

The kidneys are your body's built-in cleaning system. They use a million filters called nephrons to separate waste out of your blood so it can be released when you go to the toilet. Your body uses this system up to 60 times a day.

A LIVER, NOT A FIGHTER

The liver has an astonishing skill—it is the only internal organ that can regenerate itself. It only needs about 25 percent of the original liver to grow back to its full size.

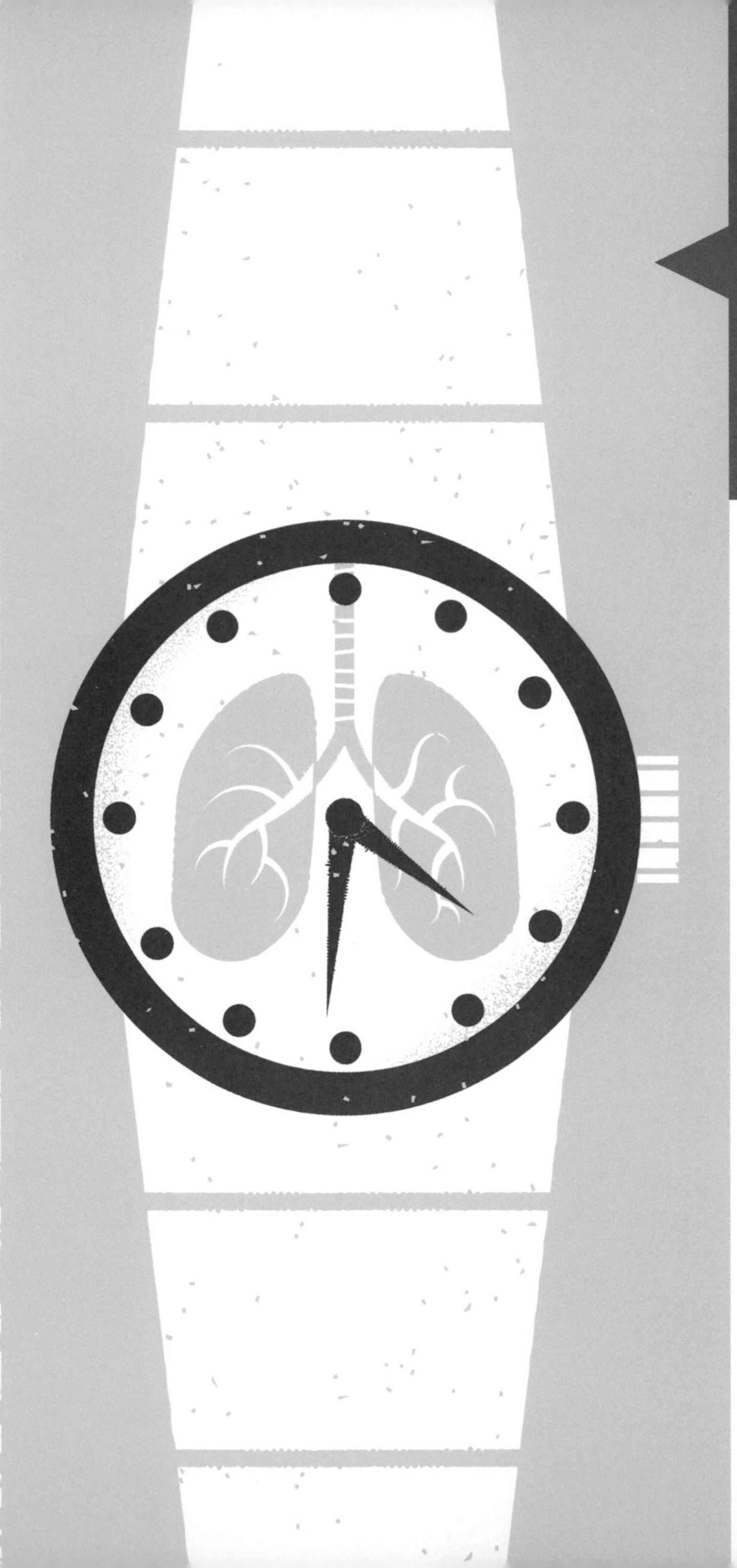

TAKE MY BREATH AWAY

A person takes about 23,040 breaths in the course of a day. Across a lifetime, that can add up to a total of 672,768,000. After special practice and training, a few swimmers can hold their breath for five long minutes.

A SQUASH AND A SQUEEZE

Your lungs are not the same size. The right lung is shorter to make room for the liver, which sits directly beneath it. The left lung is narrower, so that there is enough space for the heart.

HOLD UP

How does holding your breath work to stop hiccups? The source of the hiccups is the diaphragm spasming. Not exhaling is thought to build up the carbon dioxide in your body and stop the movement of your diaphragm.

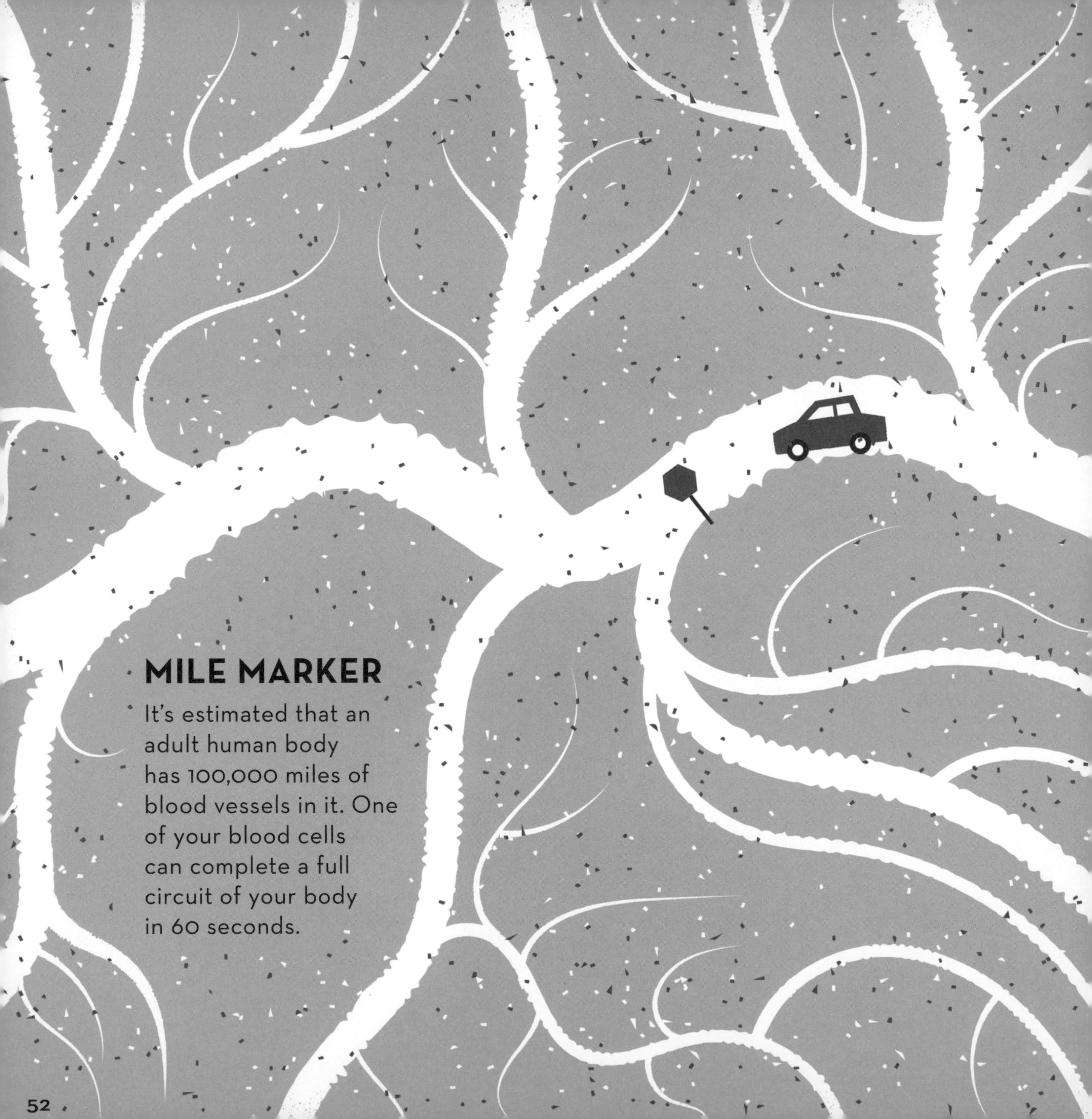

MILE MARKER

It's estimated that an adult human body has 100,000 miles of blood vessels in it. One of your blood cells can complete a full circuit of your body in 60 seconds.

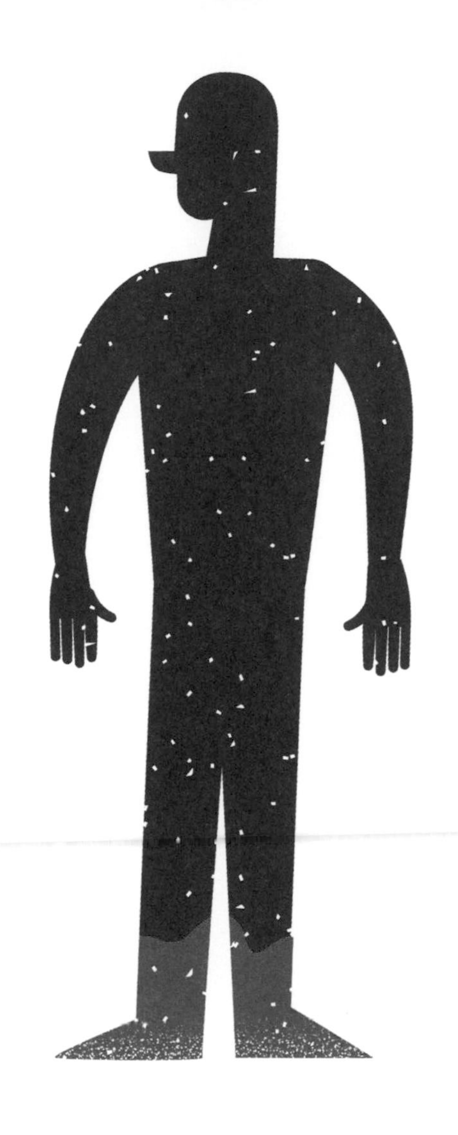

BLOOD DRIVE

The volume of blood inside you makes up 7–9 percent of your entire body weight.

RED AND WHITE

Your blood is made up of red blood cells, white blood cells, and platelets, carried along in a liquid called plasma. White blood cells defend the body against bacteria and viruses. Red blood cells deliver oxygen. Platelets help your blood to clot.

FUEL PUMP

You would have to leave your kitchen faucet running for at least 45 years to equal the amount of blood pumped by your heart in a lifetime.

FROM THE BOTTOM OF MY HEART

Your heart can build up enough pressure to squirt your blood nearly 30 feet into the air. That is higher than most two-story houses.

HEARTBEATS

An adult heart beats 72 times a minute—that is 100,000 times in a day, 3,600,000 times a year, and 2.5 billion times from birth to death. Scientists now know that your heartbeat changes its tempo to mimic the rhythm of the music you are listening to.

SAFE AND SOUND

It has been discovered that music can reduce discomfort and anxiety during hospital stays. Even unconscious patients who have music playing during surgery claim to experience less pain than those who did not.

CLINGING ON

Newborns instinctively hold on tight. A baby's grip is strong enough to support its entire body weight.

BABY BLUES

Most Caucasian babies are born with blue eyes. As they grow, the amount of melanin in their eyes builds up to bring out their true eye color.

NO BONES ABOUT IT

Babies have around 300 bones inside their little bodies. By the time they reach adulthood, the number has shrunk to 206. Some bones, such as those in the skull, fuse together as children grow older.

MADE OF STEEL

Our largest and hardest bone is the femur in the leg. It can support 30 times the weight of a person's body. The thighbone is also the longest bone and stronger than steel, ounce for ounce.

PRETTY FLY

The shortest human bone is called the stapes. Tucked inside our middle ear and measuring less than 1/12 inch, it is smaller than a housefly.

UNATTACHED

The hyoid, a small, horseshoe-shape bone in your throat, is the only bone that is not connected to any other. The hyoid adds support when you move your tongue to speak or swallow your food.

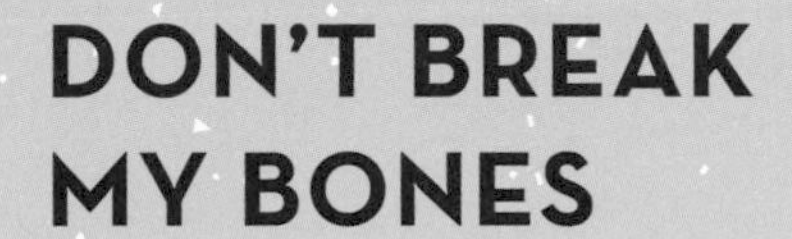

DON'T BREAK MY BONES

Bones are strong. One 2-inch chunk can support more than 9 tons of weight. That's four times harder than the concrete used to make a sidewalk.

WAT-ER YOU MADE OF?

Although hard, 31 percent of the composition of your bones is actually water.

A WHOLE NEW YOU?

Every seven to ten years, a human skeleton renews the cells inside itself completely.

WAIT A MINUTE

Nearly 300 million cells die inside the body every minute. This seems like a lot, but it is not so bad—we have 50-100 trillion cells, on average, in total.

WEIGHS A SKELE-TON

Our skeleton makes up 15 percent of our body weight, A child who weighs 60 pounds has a skeleton that weighs about 9 pounds.

TALL ORDER

The tallest person ever recorded was Robert Pershing Wadlow. When he was last measured, in 1940, he was a towering 8 feet 11 inches tall. When he stretched his arms out wide, they were 9 feet 5 3⁄4 inches long.

RECORD HEIGHT

The shortest person ever recorded was Chandra Bahadur Dangi of Nepal. His height has been recorded at 21 1⁄2 inches.

FAST TIMES

A fit human can sprint at speeds of more than 20 miles per hour, but the Olympian Usain Bolt has notched up readings in excess of 27 miles an hour—that is faster than a roadrunner.

UNDER PRESSURE

There are 1.1 tons of air pressure pushing down on your body at all times.

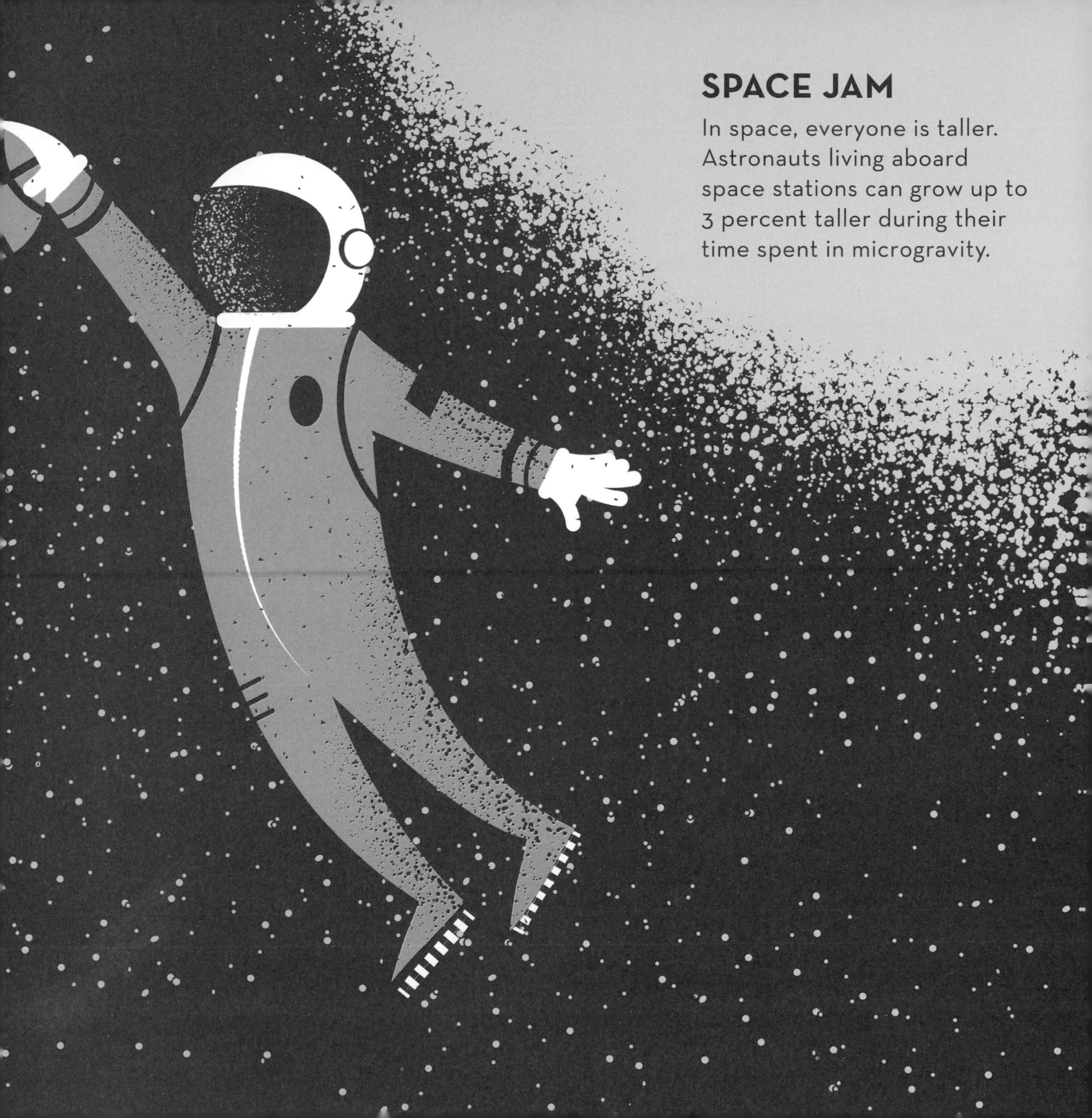

SPACE JAM

In space, everyone is taller. Astronauts living aboard space stations can grow up to 3 percent taller during their time spent in microgravity.

DEPENDING ON TENDONS

The tendons in our fingers are moved by muscles located in each forearm. Fingers themselves do not contain any muscles to move them.

SMALL BUT MIGHTY

The humble little finger contributes to half of the hand's strength. The index, middle fingers, and thumb are used in grabbing. The little finger teams up with the ring finger to support the hand.

TOUCHDOWN

Fingers are so sensitive they can feel nano-size bumps and wrinkles on a seemingly smooth surface. If your finger was the size of Earth, you would have the ability to feel the houses and even parked cars.

BONE UP!

Skulls are similar to fingerprints. The print from the part of the skull where the nose used to be is unique to each individual.

IM-PRINT

British scientists have found that the reason we have fingerprints is to wick water off our fingertips and let our skin stretch more easily. This protects our hands from damage. Fingerprints may also improve our sense of touch.

PRINT-MATES

Besides primates and people, koalas are the only other animals to have unique fingerprints.

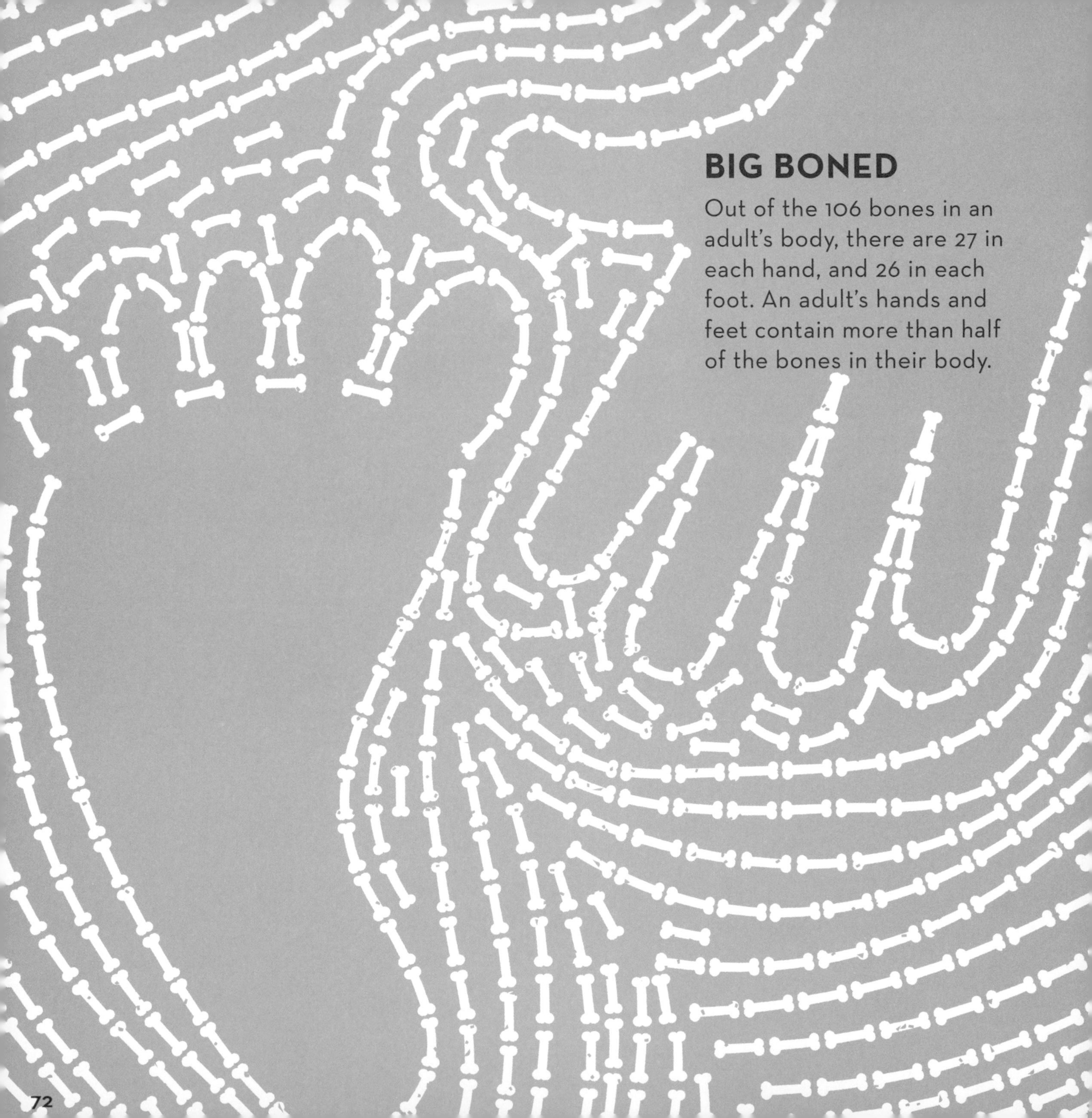

BIG BONED

Out of the 106 bones in an adult's body, there are 27 in each hand, and 26 in each foot. An adult's hands and feet contain more than half of the bones in their body.

KEEP ON TRUCKIN'

Studies have shown that, on average, a person will walk far enough in their lifetime to circumnavigate Earth five times.

OUT OF STEP

A person can use up to 200 different muscles to make a single stride.

DRIPPING WITH SWEAT

In an average pair of feet, there are 250,000 sweat glands. These glands can produce almost 1 ¼ cups of sweat a day.

BY THE FOOT

The tendons and ligaments in a person's feet loosen up as they get older, which can cause them to get bigger.

DUST IN THE WIND

We lose 600,000 particles of skin in an hour. The dust in Earth's atmosphere comes from dead human skin.

HAVE A STRETCH

Your largest organ is your skin. If you could stretch out the skin of an average adult male, it would cover around 22 square feet.

HOME SWEET HOME

There are millions of bacteria per square inch that live on the surface of your skin. The majority of these are harmless and some are even helpful to your health and well-being.

CURE ALL

Scientists have created antibiotics to fight off different diseases using bacteria found within the human body.

CAN YOU BELIEVE IT?

You carry around 3 to 5 pounds of bacteria inside your body. If you could collect them all, up you would be able to fill a large can of soup.

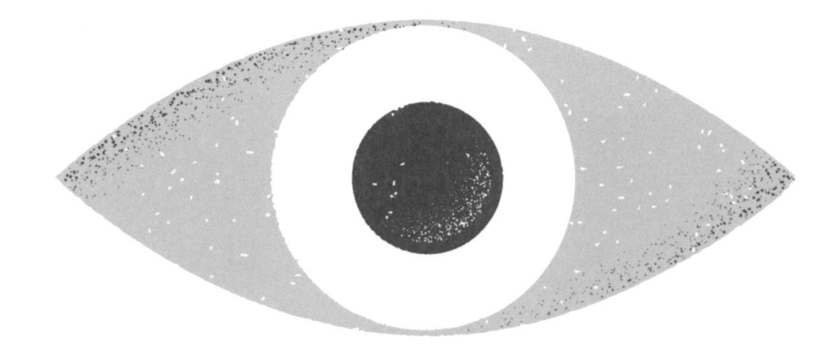

STERLING CHILDREN'S BOOKS
New York

An Imprint of Sterling Publishing Co., Inc.
1166 Avenue of the Americas
New York, NY 10036

First Sterling edition published in 2019.
First published in the United Kingdom in 2019 by Pavilion Children's Books.

ISBN 978-1-4549-3759-3
Distributed in Canada by Sterling Publishing Co., Inc.
c/o Canadian Manda Group, 664 Annette Street
Toronto, Ontario M6S 2C8, Canada
For information about custom editions, special sales, and premium and corporate purchases,
please contact Sterling Special Sales at 800-805-5489 or
specialsales@sterlingpublishing.com.
Manufactured in China
Lot #:
2 4 6 8 10 9 7 5 3 1
07/19
sterlingpublishing.com